Dirty Science

Shar Levine and Leslie Johnstone

illustrated by Lorenzo Del Bianco

25 Experiments with Soil

SCHOLASTIC CANADA LTD.
Toronto New York London Auckland Sydney
Mexico City New Delhi Hong Kong Buenos Aires

Scholastic Canada Ltd.
604 King Street West, Toronto, Ontario M5V 1E1, Canada

Scholastic Inc.
557 Broadway, New York, NY 10012, USA

Scholastic Australia Pty Limited
PO Box 579, Gosford, NSW 2250, Australia

Scholastic New Zealand Limited
Private Bag 94407, Botany, Manukau 2163, New Zealand

Scholastic Children's Books
Euston House, 24 Eversholt Street, London NW1 1DB, UK

In loving memory of Elsa and Harry Rosenberg.
—Shar

Emily and Chris: Congratulations!
—Leslie

Acknowledgements
Our thanks to the following people for their expert advice and assistance:
Murray Isman, Dean and Professor (Entomology/Toxicology) Faculty of Land and Food Systems, University of British Columbia; Dr. Maja Krzic, Associate Professor Faculty of Forestry / Faculty of Land and Food Systems, University of British Columbia; Dr. Sandra Brown, Lecturer and Research Associate, Soil Science / Applied Biology, Faculty of Land and Food Systems, University of British Columbia; Carl Zimmer

Library and Archives Canada Cataloguing in Publication

Levine, Shar, 1953-
Dirty science : 25 experiments with soil / by Shar Levine and
Leslie Johnstone ; illustrations by Lorenzo Del Bianco.

ISBN 978-1-4431-1354-0

1. Soils--Experiments--Juvenile literature. I. Johnstone, Leslie
II. Del Bianco, Lorenzo III. Title.

S591.3.L49 2013   j631.4078   C2012-907799-2

Text copyright © 2013 by Shar Levine and Leslie Johnstone.
Illustrations copyright © 2013 by Scholastic Canada Ltd.
All rights reserved.

No part of this publication may be reproduced or stored in a retrieval system, or transmitted in any form or by any means, electronic, mechanical, recording, or otherwise, without written permission of the publisher, Scholastic Canada Ltd., 604 King Street West, Toronto, Ontario M5V 1E1, Canada. In the case of photocopying or other reprographic copying, a licence must be obtained from Access Copyright (Canadian Copyright Licensing Agency), 1 Yonge Street, Suite 800, Toronto, Ontario M5E 1E5 (1-800-893-5777).

6 5 4 3 2 1   Printed in Canada 116   13 14 15 16 17

Table of Contents

Introduction 4
Note to Parents and Teachers 5
1. The Dirt on Soil 6
2. Smooth Move 8
3. In Particular 10
4. Look Sideways 12
5. Neutral Ground 14
6. Plan B. 16
7. Colour Change 18
8. Under Foot 20
9. Blown in the Wind 22
10. Losing it 24
11. You Crack Me Up. 25
12. Weather You Like it or Not 26
13. Break Down 28
14. Spongy Soil 30
15. Stalking Celery. 31
16. Down the Drain 32
17. Soft Rocks 34
18. Charcoal Filters 36
19. Grow Up! 38
20. Hydroponics. 40
21. Air-Rating. 42
22. Full of Holes. 43
23. Clay Baking 44
24. Rolling Stones 46
25. Survival 101 47
Glossary 48

Introduction

Don't be confused by the title of this book. Most people think **soil** and **dirt** are the same thing, but a pedologist, or person who studies soil, will tell you that they are quite different.

Soil is an ecosystem — the soil beneath our feet contains not only rocks and **minerals**, but also worms, insects, **bacteria**, **fungi** and plants, as well as the water, air, and rotting plant and animal matter needed to keep them alive. Soil that has only inorganic material is called dirt.

In this book you will learn interesting things about the soil between your toes and how life on Earth could not exist without it.

Soils provide the food that plants and trees need in order to grow. Water and air can be purified by filtering or being passed through soil. People use soil to make roads and buildings, and even cook with it. And, of course, earthworms, moles and other creatures consider soil a place to dig in and call home.

Get ready to get messy!

REMEMBER:

Always ask a parent before digging in a garden or on a property. Also, don't eat anything in these experiments unless instructed to do so.

NOTE TO PARENTS AND TEACHERS

In poetry and prose the words "soil," "dirt," "ground," "earth" and even "dust" may be used interchangeably. Science, on the other hand, is very specific and scientific words have precise meanings. It is always good practice to use words with scientific definitions correctly.

The science of soil is complex, and this book just scratches the surface, so to speak. Obviously we could not go into great detail about every tiny aspect of soil formation, composition and conservation. The experiments here are meant to be fun and a general introduction to the world beneath our feet. Teachers can use this as part of a lesson plan on earth science, and parents can easily try these activities at home without purchasing expensive materials.

Let's dig into science!

1. The Dirt on Soil

You might think that all dirt is the same, but did you know that soils are unique, just like fingerprints? All soils are made up of the same kinds of material, but some soils have more or less of these materials. Let's look at how we can learn to identify different types of soil.

You Will Need

- an adult helper
- a trowel
- a 500 mL (2 cup) measuring cup
- 3 or 4 soil samples from different parts of a garden, forest, park or field
- a resealable plastic bag
- a marker
- a newspaper
- a magnifying glass
- a sieve
- a pencil or pen
- a notebook

What to Do

1. Using your trowel, collect about 500 mL (2 cups) of soil from different places.
2. Place each sample in a resealable plastic bag and label it with the location from which you took it. Take your samples home.
3. Put a piece of newspaper on a table. Place one of the soil samples into the sieve. Tap or shake the sieve over the piece of paper until the soil stops falling onto the paper.
4. Use a magnifying glass to study the soil on the paper and the material left in the sieve. What colour is the soil? What kinds of rocks or materials are left in the sieve? Are there any bugs, worms or other materials in the sieve? How much soil passed through the sieve?
5. Record your observations in a notebook. Repeat steps 3 to 5 with your other samples. Were there differences?

WHAT HAPPENED?

You saw that not all soil is the same. Depending on where you gathered your soil, you may have noticed that one sample contained lots of sand, while another contained more grass and roots. Soil is a mixture of **organic materials**, inorganic materials, air and water. The organic materials in your soil may have included plants, insects or worms, decomposing leaves or bacteria. The inorganic materials in the soil are the rocks and minerals found in sand, silt and **clay**.

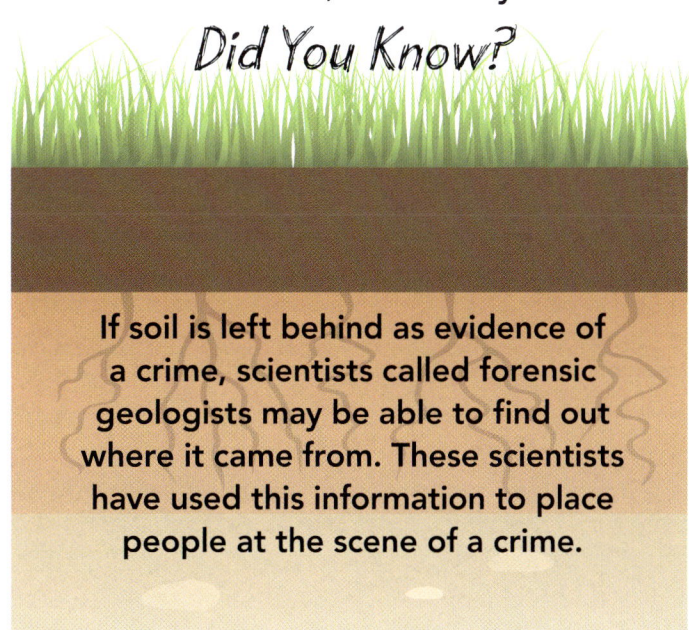

Did You Know?

If soil is left behind as evidence of a crime, scientists called forensic geologists may be able to find out where it came from. These scientists have used this information to place people at the scene of a crime.

2. Smooth Move

Now that you know that soils are unique, what kind of soil is beneath your feet? Scientists have created a way to quickly and simply classify this material without using fancy laboratory equipment. Let's see how they do it.

You Will Need

- clumps of soil from different areas (garden, forest, field, etc.)
- water
- paper
- a pen

What to Do

1. Take a handful of soil and add a drop or two of water. Roll this between your fingers. Keep adding small amounts of water until the soil feels moist.

2. Try to form a ball with the soil. Does the ball hold together or does it break apart? If it breaks apart, try adding a bit more water if it feels dry, or more soil if it feels wet. If it feels moist and still breaks apart, your soil contains mostly sand.

3. If your soil forms a ball, roll it between your palms and make it into a worm shape. If it can't be formed into a worm shape, it is a coarse loamy sand.

4. Try forming your worm shape into a ring. Does it break apart or form a ring? Soils with more clay in them will more easily form a ring. Soils that break apart are loamy soils.

5. Wet a smaller piece of the soil even more. Describe the feel of the wet soil. Does it feel smooth like butter or more like crunchy peanut butter? Smoother soils are silty; coarse-grained soils are sandy.

6. Repeat these steps with each soil sample. How does each soil sample compare?

WHAT HAPPENED?

You were able to classify your soil sample by its texture. The texture of soil is important because it allows you to pick the best soil for specific goals. Sandy soils are good as a base for building roads and buildings. The best soil for growing plants is made up of about one part of clay mixed with two parts of sand and two parts of silt. Together these three materials are known as **loam**. There are twelve ways to classify soils. "Texture" is the word used to describe the proportions of sand, clay and silt in a soil.

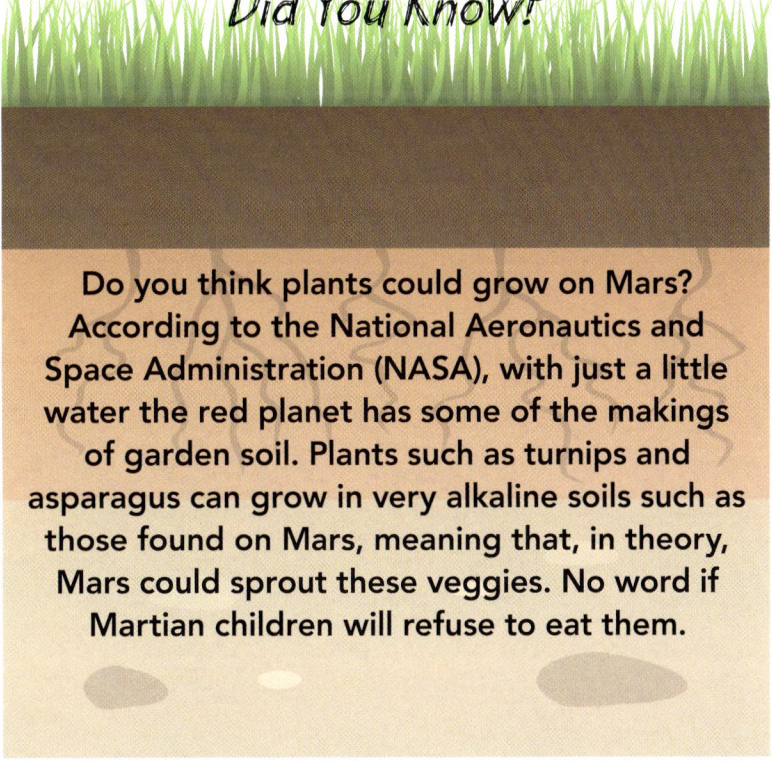

Did You Know?

Do you think plants could grow on Mars? According to the National Aeronautics and Space Administration (NASA), with just a little water the red planet has some of the makings of garden soil. Plants such as turnips and asparagus can grow in very alkaline soils such as those found on Mars, meaning that, in theory, Mars could sprout these veggies. No word if Martian children will refuse to eat them.

3. In Particular

In "Smooth Move" (page 8) you learned to classify soils based on their texture. In this activity you will see that there's more to soil than just how it feels.

You Will Need

- 3 clear, cylindrical plastic bottles with lids (wide-mouthed juice bottles work best)
- water
- potting soil
- sand
- small clumps of soil taken from a garden or lawn
- measuring cups

What to Do

1. Fill the first bottle about ⅔ full with water. Place 125 mL (½ cup) of potting soil into it and then fill it to the top with water. Tightly screw on the lid. Label this bottle "1." Shake it, mixing the soil and water and then leave it on a flat surface.

2. Fill the second bottle about ⅔ full with water. Mix 60 mL (¼ cup) of potting soil with 60 mL (¼ cup) of sand, then add this to the bottle of water. Fill the bottle to the top with water and screw on the lid. Label this bottle "2." Give this bottle a good shake and place it next to the first bottle.

3. Fill the third bottle ⅔ full with water. Drop in a clump of soil taken from a garden or lawn (about 125 mL or ½ cup), then fill the bottle with water and cap it. Label this bottle "3." Give the bottle a good shake and place it next to the other two bottles.

4. Leave the bottles overnight to allow the solids to settle. Watch what happens to the materials in the bottles. Can you see different layers?

WHAT HAPPENED?

You saw different layers of minerals in your bottles. Shaking the soils in water allowed the particles of the soil to move apart. The largest particles sank the fastest in the water, and the smallest particles took longer to sink. The particles of sand settled to the bottom. Silt, made up of the next-largest particles, was layered on top of the sand. Clay particles are the smallest, and they formed the top layer of your sample. Knowing what kind of layers the ground is made up of is important: if you are building a bridge or a home and the ground has too much sand, it makes the ground beneath these structures unstable and could cause them to collapse.

Did You Know?

When science writer Carl Zimmer volunteered to be part of a study of belly button lint, he discovered that his navel contained a species of the *Georgenia* bacteria previously found only in soil in Japan. This was surprising as he had never visited that country.

4. Look Sideways

Take a walk around your neighbourhood. Is there a construction site or a hillside with an exposed side where you can see the layers of the soil below the ground? How many layers do you see? Soil is usually made up of several layers. Let's make an edible soil profile.

You Will Need

- an adult helper
- a disposable aluminum loaf pan (or a loaf pan lined with aluminum foil)
- graham crackers
- marshmallows
- chocolate ice cream or other frozen treat
- vanilla ice cream or other frozen treat
- 250 mL (1 cup) chocolate chips
- a microwaveable bowl
- chocolate wafer crumbs
- a sharp knife

What to Do

1. Lay the graham crackers in the bottom of the loaf pan.
2. Put a layer of marshmallows on top of the crackers.
3. Allow the chocolate ice cream to soften so it can be stirred with a spoon. Then spoon a layer of it over the marshmallows so they are completely covered. Put the pan into the freezer and allow the ice cream layer to harden.
4. Allow the vanilla ice cream to soften so it can be stirred with a spoon. Then spoon a thick layer of ice cream over the chocolate ice cream. Put the pan into the freezer and allow the ice cream layer to harden.
5. Place the chocolate chips in a microwaveable bowl and have an adult use the microwave to just melt the chips. Spread the melted chocolate over the top of the vanilla ice cream.
6. Sprinkle chocolate wafer crumbs over the melted chocolate. Put the pan into the freezer until the chocolate is hard.
7. Remove the ice cream treat from the freezer and carefully remove it from the pan. Have an adult use a sharp knife dipped in hot water to cut a slice. You have an ice cream profile.

WHAT HAPPENED?

You created a soil profile model with ice cream representing the different layers you might find if you dug deep into the soil in your backyard. Starting from the top: the chocolate crumbs represent **humus**, the organic material, such as leaves and plants, on the soil surface. Below that, the vanilla ice cream is the topsoil layer, which contains both organic and inorganic materials necessary for plant growth. Next, the chocolate ice cream represents the subsoil layers of minerals with a smaller amount of organic material. The marshmallows are the layer of bedrock and rock fragments called parent material. Finally, you come to graham crackers, which are the bedrock layer of the soil. Now dig in!

5. Neutral Ground

Plants grow better in some soils than in others. Sea asparagus grows well in areas with salty soil that would kill most other plants. Succulents thrive in sandy plots with good drainage. Roses prefer a rich dark soil with lots of organic material and a slightly **acidic** soil. We measure acidity using the **pH** scale — the lower the pH number, the more acidic the soil is. Let's learn how acidic your soil is.

You Will Need

- a garden
- a trowel or small shovel
- a 500 mL (2 cup) measuring cup
- measuring spoons
- pH testing strips (available at garden or aquarium stores)
- a bottle of distilled water (found at grocery stores)
- 2 plastic containers with lids
- soil
- coffee filters

What to Do

1. Find a spot in the garden and use a trowel or small shovel to remove leaves and twigs from the surface. Dig up about 250 mL (1 cup) of topsoil. Remove any twigs, rocks, plants, bugs or worms from the cup. Place this sample in a plastic container, break up any clumps in the soil and mix it well.

2. Add about 60 mL (¼ cup) of the soil to another plastic container. Add 60 mL (¼ cup) of distilled water to the container. Do not use tap water as it may not be pH neutral.

3. Place a lid on the container and shake it.

4. Put it on a flat surface and allow the soil to settle.

5. When the water at the top of the container is mostly clear, put a coffee filter into the water and press down to trap some filtered liquid. Place the end of a pH test strip in this liquid. Match the colour of the pH strip to the colour chart provided with the strips.

6. Try this again using soil from a different part of the garden or soil taken from a forest, park or field. Is the pH the same as the soil around your home?

WHAT HAPPENED?

If the colour on the pH strip was yellow or orange, your sample was acidic. Green meant the sample was **neutral**, and dark green meant it was **alkaline**. The pH of soils you tested may have ranged from less than 7 (acidic) to more than 7 (alkaline). Neutral soil has a pH of 7. Much like people have food preferences, plants also like certain kinds of soil. Tomatoes grow best in slightly acidic soil with a pH of 5.5–7. Lettuce plants will die in soil that is too acidic, but planting blueberries in this kind of soil will give you baskets of fruit. Knowing the pH of the soil helps gardeners and farmers plant the kinds of crops or plants best suited for the soil.

6. Plan B

Now that you know the pH of the soil in your garden, is it possible to change the pH to make the soil more alkaline or more acidic?

You Will Need

- water
- a measuring cup
- measuring spoons
- 4 small plastic containers with lids
- pH testing strips (available at pharmacies, garden centres or aquarium stores)
- a pen
- paper
- vinegar
- baking soda
- soil
- a marker

What to Do

1. Label the containers from 1 to 4 and place 125 mL (½ cup) of water in each one. Place the end of a pH test strip in this liquid. Match the colour of the pH strip to the colour chart. Record the pH of each sample.

2. Add 30 mL (2 tbsp) of vinegar to the first container. Measure and record the pH of the mixture with a pH testing strip.

3. Add 30 mL (2 tbsp) of baking soda to the second container. Put the lid on the container and shake it well. Measure and record the pH of the mixture with a pH testing strip.

4. Add 60 mL (¼ cup) of soil to each of the third and fourth containers. Put the lids on the containers and shake them well. Allow the soil to settle until the liquid at the top of the container is clear. Measure and record the pH of the mixture with a pH testing strip.

5. Add 30 mL (2 tbsp) of vinegar to the third container and 30 mL (2 tbsp) of baking soda to the fourth container. Put the lids on the containers and shake them well. Allow the soil to settle until the liquid at the top of the container is clear. Measure and record the pH of the mixtures with a pH testing strip.

WHAT HAPPENED?

You learned how to change the pH in your soil. Adding vinegar and baking soda changed the pH of the water. The vinegar made the pH in the water decrease, or become more acidic, because it is an acid. The baking soda made the pH increase, or become more alkaline, because it is a **base**. When you added vinegar and baking soda to the soil mixture, you didn't get as large a change in the pH as when you added it to the water. This is because soil acts as a buffer. Buffers are mixtures that absorb acids and bases so that the pH doesn't change as much.

7. Colour Change

You know that the leaves on trees change colour in the fall, but is it possible for a plant to change the colour of its flowers? With a little patience and science you can make a pink flower blue and a blue flower pink.

Will Need

- a small potted pink hydrangea (available in the spring)
- a small potted blue hydrangea (available in the spring)
- measuring spoons
- dolomite lime (available at aquarium stores or garden centres)
- coffee grounds
- dry pine needles
- a trowel or small spoon

NOTE: Do not use a white hydrangea for this activity as it will not change colour. Plants in larger containers will take longer to change colour than plants in smaller pots.

What to Do

1. Use the spoon or trowel to mix coffee 15ml (1 tbsp) of grounds into the soil of the pink hydrangea. Cover the soil with a sprinkling of pine needles, and water the plant.
2. Add 15 mL (1 tbsp) of dolomite lime to the pot with the blue hydrangea and use the spoon or trowel to mix it into the soil. Water the plant.
3. Once a week, add 15 mL (1 tbsp) of coffee grounds to the pink plant and 15 mL (1 tbsp) of dolomite lime to the blue plant.
4. Watch the flowers on each plant.

WHAT HAPPENED?

Within a few months your pink hydrangea flowers turned blue, and your blue hydrangea flowers turned pink. Hydrangeas contain coloured chemicals or **pigments** called **anthocyanins**. The same anthocyanin can be pink or blue depending on the amount of aluminum in the plant. The coffee grounds made the soil more acidic which allowed the plant to take up more aluminum and made the pigment blue. Instead of adding coffee, some people add pickle juice — which contains vinegar and sometimes additional aluminum. Adding dolomite lime to the soil made it more alkaline which reduced the aluminum in the flowers and made the pigment pink.

8. Under Foot

Each time you slide for a base while playing ball, run through the lawn to catch a Frisbee or simply take a stroll through the forest, you are treading on millions of microscopic creatures. Is there any way to see these little critters?

You Will Need

- an adult helper
- a 2 L plastic recyclable pop or water bottle
- scissors
- rubbing alcohol
- a 30 cm (1 ft) square piece of nylon mesh (ask if you can cut apart an old shower puff)
- an adjustable desk lamp
- fresh soil from the garden
- leaves, grass or other plant materials
- a magnifying glass
- black construction paper
- masking tape
- a white plastic lid from a container

What to Do

1. Have an adult carefully cut off the top third of the pop bottle. This is your funnel. Turn the funnel upside down and place it into the bottom part of the pop bottle. Now any liquid you pour into the funnel will collect in the bottom part.

2. Wrap the bottom of the pop bottle with black construction paper so that ⅔ of it is covered, and tape it in place.

3. Pour about 125 mL (½ cup) of rubbing alcohol into the funnel so it covers the bottom of the pop bottle.

4. Press the nylon mesh down into the funnel so it makes a bowl shaped screen to hold your soil sample. Leave a gap between the bottom of the screen bowl and the funnel. Fold the mesh over and tape it to the outside of the container to hold it in place.

5. Add enough fresh, damp soil from around your house and garden to fill the bowl about ¾ of the way to the top. Do not use potting soil from a bag. Add some plant matter over the soil. Remove any insects or worms you see in the soil.

6. Place your pop bottle with the funnel on a table and position the desk lamp over the top of the funnel. The lamp's light bulb should be about 13 cm (5 in) from the surface of the soil. You have made a Berlese funnel.

7. Leave the light shinning on the soil for two hours. Remove the construction paper from the outside of the pop bottle. What's crawling (floating) in the alcohol?

8. Place the creatures on the white plastic lid and use the magnifying glass to examine them.

9. Try this again, this time using material from a different part of the garden. Did you find the same kinds of organisms?

NOTE: You can rinse out the funnel and collector to use for the experiment "Charcoal Filters" on page 36.

WHAT HAPPENED?

You saw that there are several types of organisms in the soil, including tiny segmented animals with jointed legs called micro-arthropods. You were able to find them by using a type of Berlese funnel. The micro-arthropods moved down in your funnel to move away from the light and were trapped and preserved in the alcohol at the bottom of the bottle. Depending on your soil sample, these animals may have included very small insects, arachnids, crustaceans, centipedes and millipedes. These creatures shred leaves so they can break down to release nutrients. They can also eat other small insects, fungi and bacteria in the soil. Some of the arthropods in soil can be harmful, eating the leaves and roots of plants.

9. Blown in the Wind

There was a terrible **drought** in the 1930s in Canada and the United States. Not only did large areas of these countries dry up, but terrible winds blew across the lands, taking with them the rich topsoil. The Dust Bowl, as it was called, destroyed a quarter of all the farming land. You might think that soil doesn't move, but let's see if that's true.

You Will Need

- 3 disposable plastic cups
- dry soil
- sand
- moist soil
- a small container with a plant, with moist soil

What to Do

1. Go outside and fill one cup to the rim with dry soil, a second cup to the rim with sand and a third cup to the rim with moist soil. Do not press the soil down when you are filling the cups.
2. Hold the cup with dry soil up to your mouth so the rim is level with your lips. Take a deep breath and blow as hard as you can over the surface of the soil.
3. Repeat, this time using the cup with the sand. Repeat this using the cup with the moist soil.
4. Hold up the container with the plant and blow.
5. Compare the soil level in the cups with the sand, dry soil and moist soil with the level of soil in the container with the plant. Which container lost the most material?

WHAT HAPPENED?

You noticed that the moist soil and the one with the plant didn't lose as much soil as the dry soil and sand. Blowing across the surface of the containers was similar to a strong wind blowing over the land. Wind can remove large areas of sand and dry soil. Moisture helps the soil particles stick together. The roots of plants help to anchor the soil, and the leaves, branches and stalks of the plants break up the wind so it doesn't blow as strongly on the soil. Topsoil is rich in nutrients and helps plants grow: if plants dry out and die in a drought, they no longer hold the topsoil in place. The movement of soil materials from one location to another is called erosion.

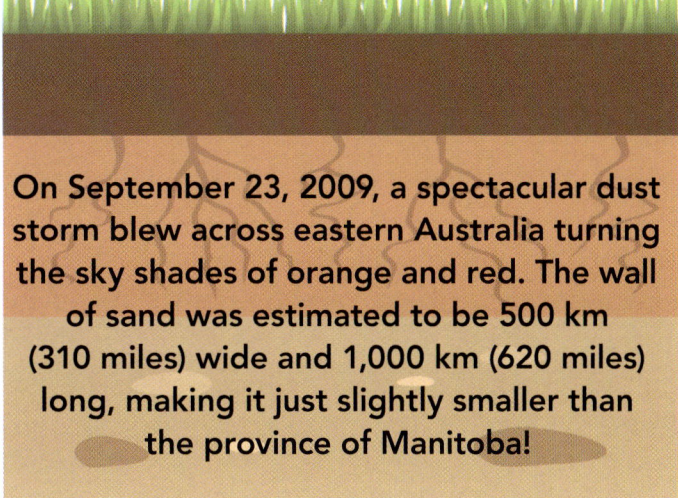

Did You Know?

On September 23, 2009, a spectacular dust storm blew across eastern Australia turning the sky shades of orange and red. The wall of sand was estimated to be 500 km (310 miles) wide and 1,000 km (620 miles) long, making it just slightly smaller than the province of Manitoba!

10. Losing it

You might think that a rainfall after a long dry spell would be welcomed. But often it is too much of a good thing. Instead of soaking into the hard, cracked earth, the water turns into a river and washes away the topsoil. Why?

You Will Need

- 3 disposable cups
- soil
- several dimes
- a watering can
- a patch of grass

What to Do

1. Fill all the cups with soil and press down on the soil to compress it. Continue adding and compressing the soil until it is even with the top of the cups.
2. Place the cups with the soil outside on a flat surface.
3. Lay several coins on top of the soil in each of the cups.
4. Holding the watering can high above the surface of the first cup, sprinkle for a few seconds to mimic a rain shower.
5. Do this again about 30 cm (1 ft) over the surface of the second cup, but water for about 15 seconds. This is like a light rain.
6. Holding the watering can close to the surface of the third cup, water the soil for about 30 seconds. This represents heavy rain.
7. Place several coins on a flat, grassy area and try this activity again. What happened?

WHAT HAPPENED?

When the water fell in a shower, the coins didn't wash away and some water was absorbed by the soil. The light rain caused some of the soil to wash away, leaving columns of soil around the coin, and again the soil took in some of the water. The heavy rain was like a flash flood, washing away the coins. When the water fell this fast, most of it didn't absorb into the soil. The area with the grass could absorb the water without disturbing the soil, and the coins didn't move. This is what happens when we get heavy rain. So after a dry spell, a light shower is better for the soil.

11. You Crack Me Up

As you have seen, soil is made up of different materials. There may be stones of different shapes, colours and sizes in the soil samples you have collected. What caused these stones to break apart into smaller pebbles?

You Will Need

- several small, clean, disposable plastic containers with lids or thin-sided clear plastic food containers
- a small cookie sheet or metal tray
- water
- a freezer

What to Do

1. Clear out enough space in your freezer to place a small cookie sheet or metal tray flat inside, with your containers on it.
2. Place the plastic containers on the tray and fill the containers to the very top with water. Put the lids on the containers.
3. Leave the containers in the freezer overnight.
4. Remove the frozen containers and take them outdoors. Drop the containers onto the sidewalk. Make sure you clean up the broken pieces of plastic.

WHAT HAPPENED?

If you are using a thin plastic container it may have cracked as the water froze and expanded in the container. Water expands when it is frozen into ice, so it takes up more space and breaks open the container. When you dropped the containers on the concrete, the plastic shattered and the ice inside cracked. In nature, water in the cracks in rocks freezes and thaws, and much like in your experiment, over time this process can cause the rocks to break apart. Rocks can also be broken down by the movement of animals and plants, by the growth of crystals and by the action of wind and water. The breakdown of rocks and minerals by these processes is called physical **weathering**.

12. Weather You Like it or Not

Where does soil come from? Nature cannot simply order a load of topsoil delivered to where it is needed. So how is it created?

You Will Need

- a piece of chalk
- a plastic bowl
- an eyedropper or teaspoon
- white vinegar
- fine steel wool (not the kind with detergent)
- gloves (to protect your hands from the steel wool)
- measuring spoons
- table salt
- 125 mL (½ cup) coarse salt
- 4 resealable plastic bags
- water
- a magnifying glass

What to Do

1. Place a small piece of chalk in a plastic bowl. Add a few drops of white vinegar to the top of the chalk with an eyedropper or teaspoon. Watch and listen carefully.

2. Put on gloves to handle the steel wool. Place a small piece of steel wool in each of the three plastic bags. Seal the first bag. Add 30 mL (2 tbsp) of water to the second bag and seal the bag. Add 5 mL (1 tsp) of table salt and 30 mL (2 tbsp) of water to the third bag and seal it. Leave the bags on a flat surface for two or three days. Examine the steel wool inside each bag.

3. Place 125 mL (½ cup) of coarse salt in the fourth plastic bag and seal the bag. Hold the bag by the sealed end and smash it for about 10 seconds against a hard surface, like the edge of a counter. Look carefully at the salt in the bag. How has it changed?

WHAT HAPPENED?

Chalk is made of chemicals that have calcium. If your chalk was mostly calcium carbonate, when the vinegar was dropped on it, it should have formed bubbles of carbon dioxide, a colourless and odourless gas. Chalk can also be made from calcium sulphate, which is not as able to react with vinegar, so you may not have heard or seen any change. When rocks react with water or acids, it is called chemical weathering. The steel wool changed in the bags with the water and the water and salt. The iron in the steel reacted with oxygen in the water. This is another example of chemical weathering. Salt helps the reaction to happen more quickly. Rocks that have a lot of iron in them usually look red due to the iron and oxygen reaction. The coarse salt also changed. It broke apart into smaller pieces as the chunks of salt banged against each other. This is an example of mechanical weathering. Mechanical weathering occurs when rocks or minerals are acted on by heat, cold, water or pressure. All of this weathering is what gives us soil.

Did You Know?

Geologists, or scientists who study the earth, have been known to lick rocks. They say that they can tell something about the rock by the way it tastes. But they don't lick the outside like a lollipop — they crack it open and lick the inside, which hasn't come in contact with people, pets or pollution.

13. Break Down

You probably don't want to eat your orange peel, but there is a creature that would love to dine on it. It will end up helping the environment at the same time. Worms (in particular red wigglers) are nature's garbage disposals. They love to eat organic materials such as fruit and vegetable peelings, apple cores or browning lettuce leaves. Let's give these wigglers a place to eat out!

You Will Need

- an adult helper
- a 20 L (5 gallon) plastic container with a lid
- a hammer and nail or a drill with a fine bit
- moss or dead leaves
- sand
- garden soil
- water
- 500 g (1 lb) red wigglers (available from bait and tackle shops or specialty shops that sell composters) or earthworms from your garden
- food garbage such as fruit and vegetable scraps and eggshells but no meat, fat, dairy products or foods with salt or sugar

What to Do

1. Have an adult hammer or drill holes every 7 or 8 centimetres (3 in) on the top, side and lid of the container. Each hole should be no larger than 3 mm (⅛ in).

2. Add a layer of moss or dead leaves to the bottom of the container.

3. Add a layer of sand on top of the moss or leaves.

4. Add enough soil to nearly fill the container. There should be enough space at the top to allow room for the castings the worms will make and to allow air.

5. Water the mixture so that it is moist but not soaked.

6. Add the worms to the container. Watch as they begin to burrow their way into the dirt.

7. Put the lid on the container.

8. Add food garbage to your composter. Larger pieces of food such as banana peels should be chopped up. Choose a different spot in the composter each time you add the food pieces. Be sure not to overfeed your worms (500 g [1 lb] of worms will eat 250 g (.5 lbs) of garbage each day). Place your composter outside in a shady place and check it every day.

9. Each month use the compost in your gardens. Gently scrape the worms to one side with the trowel when removing the compost. Then add new soil.

WHAT HAPPENED?

You made a composter. Feeding your fruit and vegetable waste to the worms not only kept garbage from filling up landfills, but it also gave you **compost**. Compost is a natural **fertilizer** that will help add nutrients to the soil in your garden. Worms help break down the organic materials to make nutrient-rich humus. They also create air pockets in the soil, helping the roots of plants to grow and take in air and water.

14. Spongy Soil

Commercials often tell you that one product is more absorbent than another. The same can be said of soils. Let's see how much water different materials are able to soak up.

You Will Need

- a 500 mL (2 cup) measuring cup
- a bowl
- water
- a small kitchen sponge
- a facecloth or dishwashing cloth

What to Do

1. Pour 500 mL (2 cups) of water into a bowl. Dip a dry sponge into the water until it is covered. Once the sponge has absorbed as much water as possible, hold it above the bowl. Allow any excess water to drip off into the bowl. Do not squeeze it.

2. Place the sponge over the empty measuring cup and squeeze as much water as you can from it back into the measuring cup. Measure the water in the cup. Record your findings.

3. Empty the measuring cup and then fill it with the water that remained in the bowl. Record your findings.

4. Calculate the amount of water that remained in the sponge by subtracting the amount of water you squeezed from the sponge and the amount that remained in the bowl from the original 500 mL (2 cups) you used.

5. Repeat steps 1 to 4 using a facecloth or a dishwashing cloth instead of the sponge.

WHAT HAPPENED?

The sponge absorbed some of the water in the bowl, but not all of it. Your facecloth or dishwashing cloth held a different amount of water than the sponge. Each item became filled with water. Soils also absorb water, and just like your materials, they can become saturated: some water is removed by plants, but not all of it. It is important for farmers to know how much water will be absorbed by the soil.

15. Stalking Celery

In the last experiment, you saw that soils absorb water that can be used by plants. How do plants soak up water from the soil?

You Will Need
- an adult helper
- a knife
- celery
- a clear drinking glass
- water
- food colouring

What to Do

1. Have the adult cut off the stem end of the celery so the bottom white portion is removed but the top leafy part remains.
2. Fill a glass with several inches of water and add a few drops of food colouring to the water.
3. Stand the celery bottom in the water. Place the glass on a flat surface and leave it for several hours.
4. Remove the celery from the glass and have an adult cut the celery crosswise in half. What did you see?

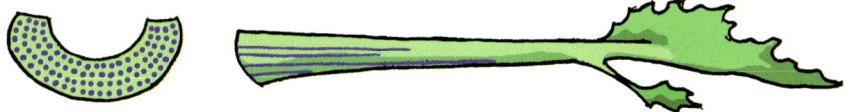

WHAT HAPPENED?

The water with the food colouring moved up the stalk of celery into the leaves. This was done through absorption, as we observed in "Spongy Soil" (page 30). From the outside, the stalk had stripes of colour. When you cut the celery crosswise in half, the stripes looked like dots of colour. Colour shows where the dye has travelled along the xylem cells of the stalk. Xylem cells transport water and dissolved nutrients from the roots of the plant in the soil into the leaves of plants. If the water or soil where a plant is growing is contaminated with pollutants, these can also be taken up by the plant just like the dye travelled up the stalk in the water.

16. Down the Drain

Not all soils are the same. Some have lots of clay while others have a thick layer of rocks or pebbles. Soils near forests might have a rich layer of humus, while others near riverbanks might be high in silt but low in nutrients. How do these differences affect the way the soil holds water?

You Will Need

- a wooden skewer or turkey skewer
- 4 large disposable cups
- a 250 mL (1 cup) measuring cup
- sand
- clay
- loamy soil (not sandy or rocky)
- gravel or pebbles
- a small bowl
- water
- your helper
- a stopwatch or watch with a second hand

What to Do

1. Use a skewer to poke five holes in the bottom of each of the large disposable cups.

2. Using the measuring cup, add 125 mL (½ cup) of sand to one cup, 125 mL (½ cup) of clay to the second cup, and 125 mL (½ cup) of loamy soil to the third cup. In the fourth cup place 60 mL (¼ cup) of gravel, and add 60 mL (¼ cup) of soil over the gravel.

3. Hold the cup with sand over a bowl and pour 250 mL (1 cup) of water into the cup. Have your helper time how long it takes the water to run through the sand. Measure the amount of water in the bowl.

4. Repeat step 3 using the cup with clay, then the cup with the soil and finally the cup with the pebbles and soil. Which cup drained the fastest? Which cup held the most water?

WHAT HAPPENED?

Water drained more quickly through the sand and the mixture of soil and gravel than it did through just soil or just clay. The ability of soil to allow water to travel through it is called its permeability. If soil is not permeable, water will not drain from it; plants growing in it can become overwatered and their roots will rot. Particles of sand are bigger than particles of clay so there are larger spaces between the particles. This makes it easier for water to travel through it. The loamy soil and the mixture of soil and gravel absorbed more of the water than the sand. These soils will store water, which can then be used by plants. They will also allow water to drain so that the plants don't become overwatered.

Did You Know?

For every 500 g (1 lb) of plant material that grows, plants need to take up 90–450 kg (200–1000 lbs) of water.

17. Soft Rocks

As you have seen, rocks can break down in different ways, including chemical weathering, freezing and thawing. But do some rocks and minerals break down more easily to form soil than others?

You Will Need

- a penny
- a common nail
- chalk or talc
- gypsum (from a building supply store)
- calcite (from a hobby store)
- a small piece of glass
- a concrete nail
- various rocks from the garden

What to Do

1. Line up the penny, the common nail, the piece of glass, and the concrete nail. These are your testers.

2. The first tester is your fingernail. Run your fingernail across a piece of chalk. Can your fingernail easily make a scratch in it?

3. Run your fingernail across a piece of gypsum. Is it as easy to make a scratch in it as it was in the chalk?

4. Try running your fingernail across a piece of calcite. Now try using a penny to make a scratch. Try scratching the glass with the penny.

5. Test each of your rock samples by using each of the testers in turn until you get a scratch on the rock. First try your fingernail, then the penny, then the common nail, then the glass, then try the concrete nail.

WHAT HAPPENED?

You discovered that it is easier to break down or scratch some of the rocks. Friedrich Mohs, an Austrian mineralogist, came up with a scale of mineral hardness in 1812. He used ten minerals as standards by which to determine the hardness of minerals and other objects. These ten minerals were arranged on a scale of increasing hardness.

MOHS SCALE

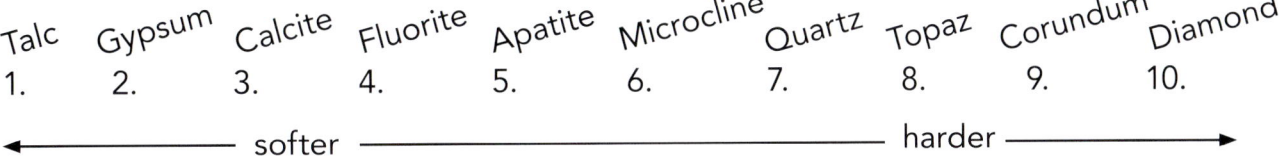

Talc	Gypsum	Calcite	Fluorite	Apatite	Microcline	Quartz	Topaz	Corundum	Diamond
1.	2.	3.	4.	5.	6.	7.	8.	9.	10.

← softer ——————————————————— harder →

Did You Know?

Diamond cutters use diamonds to cut other diamonds. They cut a groove into the diamond along a weak section of the gem and strike hard along the groove with a steel blade which splits the diamond into two pieces. Then they can saw or grind using diamonds or hard, diamond-tipped blades and grinders. Lasers can also be used to cut diamonds but this actually takes longer.

18. Charcoal Filters

People drink a lot of filtered water. But is there any way for you to make your own filtered water?

NOTE: Do not drink the water you have filtered. Throw it away after the experiment and have an adult thoroughly clean the kitchenware you used.

You Will Need

- an adult helper
- clean, small pebbles
- 2 L plastic pop or water bottle (or the Berlese funnel from "Under Foot" on page 20)
- scissors
- a coffee filter or piece of paper towel
- crushed and washed activated charcoal (available at pet stores)
- clean, fine sand
- clean, coarse sand
- cotton balls
- different colours of food colouring
- water
- a drinking glass
- a rolling pin

What to Do

1. Rinse your pebbles until the water you're rinsing them in is completely clear.
2. Have an adult use scissors to carefully cut off the top third of the pop bottle. This is your funnel. Turn the funnel upside down and place it into the bottom part of the pop bottle. Now any liquid you pour into the funnel will collect in the bottom part.
3. Place the coffee filter or paper towel into the funnel.
4. Place a layer of cotton balls in the bottom of the paper filter.
5. Add a 2 cm (¾ inch) layer of small pebbles on top of the cotton balls.
6. Place a 2 cm (¾ inch) layer of coarse sand on top of the small pebbles.
7. Place a 2 cm (¾ inch) layer of fine sand on top of the coarse sand.
8. Rinse the charcoal under running water, then use a rolling pin to crush it. Make sure the charcoal is finely crushed, then add a bit of water to it to make a paste, and place this on top of the fine sand. You have made a filter.

9. Stir some of each food colouring into a glass of water. Pour 250 mL (1 cup) of coloured water into the filter and watch as it drains through the filter into the collector.

10. If you wish, take the filtered water from step 9 and run it through the filter again. Was it different the second time?

11. Throw away the water, sand, charcoal, pebbles, coffee filter and cotton balls.

WHAT HAPPENED?

You made your own water filter. The filter removed some of the colour from the water. After draining through the five layers, the water became less coloured. Food colouring is made up of particles, which are **adsorbed** by (attached to) the charcoal. Some colours were adsorbed better than others. The pebbles and sand create small pockets of air that keep the charcoal from clumping up and blocking the filter. Soils act as filters by removing impurities in the same way as you removed the colours from your water sample.

19. Grow Up!

Your body needs the right kinds of nutrients to help you grow strong bones and keep you healthy. But do plants also need nutrients to keep them growing big and strong?

You Will Need

- masking tape
- a pen
- 3 identical planters
- 3 identical small plants such as lettuce, cress or parsley
- potting soil
- commercial plant fertilizer found in supermarkets or plant stores
- compost (see "Break Down" from page 28)
- water
- paper or a digital camera

What to Do

1. Use masking tape and a pen to label the planters as follows: Plant 1=Water; Plant 2=Compost; Plant 3=Fertilizer.

2. Place a plant in potting soil in planter 1 and only use tap water to keep this plant moist.

3. Place a plant with a mixture of potting soil and compost in planter 2 and use tap water to keep this plant moist.

4. Place a plant with potting soil in planter 3 and use the fertilizer and tap water to keep this plant moist.

5. Place the planters on a flat surface in the sun and watch them grow for several weeks. Each day, make sure the plants are moist. Record the height of the plants, the number of leaves and the size of the leaves. Which plant grew the most? Which one the least?

WHAT HAPPENED?

If all the other factors such as sunlight and water were the same, the plant with the fertilizer should have grown the most. Commercial fertilizers have three important nutrients for plant growth: nitrogen, phosphorus and potassium. The amounts of each of these are shown on the container. For example, the numbers for your fertilizer might be 12–5–4. This means that the fertilizer contains 12% nitrogen, 5% phosphorus and 4% potassium. Nitrogen helps plants produce their green pigment, chlorophyll, which allows them to grow more rapidly. Phosphorus is important for producing strong roots and lots of flowers. Potassium helps to protect plants from diseases and extreme weather. Compost also contains these nutrients but in much smaller amounts than commercial fertilizer. The advantage of using compost in your garden is that it also contains the organic material and microorganisms that the soil needs to stay healthy with proper watering.

20. Hydroponics

Here's a great activity that combines recycling, botany, water conservation and soil science. You are going to make your own tiny **hydroponic** garden. The word hydroponic comes from the Greek stems "hydro," which means water, and "ponos," which means work or labour. So, let's let the water do the work.

You Will Need

- an adult helper
- a clear, clean 2 L pop or water bottle with cap
- scissors
- perlite (available in a garden store)
- a small plant
- hydroponic solution or powdered fertilizer (found in a garden store)
- an old cotton t-shirt
- bottled water

What to Do

1. Have an adult use sharp scissors to cut the soda bottle in half. The top portion of the bottle is your "planter." The bottom will be your water container. Leave the cap on the bottle top.

2. Use a pair of scissors to cut a strip of fabric 4 cm (1.5 in) wide and 10 cm (4 in) long from an old cotton t-shirt. This is your wick.

3. Have the adult use scissors to make a small horizontal slit, about 5 cm (2 in) wide, close to the neck of the bottle. This is where your wick will go.

4. Thread one end of the wick through the slit in the planter.

5. Place your planter inside the container, with the bottle top facing downward. The wick should touch the bottom of the container.

6. Fill the planter just about to the top with perlite. Put your plant into the perlite.

7. Follow the instructions on the hydroponic solution or add 1 mL (¼ tsp) of powdered fertilizer to a litre of bottled water. Pour the solution or the water with the fertilizer over the planter and keep pouring until the water has drained through the planter and has filled the container with 5 cm (2 in) of water.

8. Place the planter on a flat surface where it will get some sunlight (but not direct sunlight). Keep the planter moist by adding a bit more water if needed.

WHAT HAPPENED?

You were able to grow a plant without using soil. Using the wick, the roots of the plant were able to pull up nutrients from the liquid you used. Hydroponic solutions contain nitrogen, phosphorus and potassium as well as other nutrients that plants require for proper growth. If you used fertilizer instead of hydroponic solution, your plant may have been lacking some of the nutrients it needed to grow as quickly and to be as healthy as possible.

21. Air-Rating

You know that soil is alive. It contains organisms such as bacteria, insects and worms. What else might you expect to find in soil? Here's a hint: take a deep breath.

You Will Need

- an adult helper
- a field, lawn or park
- an apple corer
- a plastic bag
- 3 tall, clear glasses
- potting soil
- water

What to Do

1. Find a small, green patch of grass. Have an adult use the apple corer to remove a sample core of grass and soil and place it in the plastic bag. Try to keep the sample core in one piece and inside the corer.

2. Fill a tall, clear glass with water. Remove the corer from the plastic bag. Carefully push the sample from the apple corer directly into the water. Watch as the sample falls to the bottom of the glass. Can you see bubbles rise?

3. Try it again, this time using a sample taken from a different location. Place it into a glass with clean water. Can you see a difference between the two samples?

4. Take a sample of potting soil from a bag and place it into a third glass of clean water. Is there a difference between the potting soil and the soil from the grass?

WHAT HAPPENED?

Depending on where you took your sample and the age of the soil, you probably saw tiny bubbles rising as the soil sank to the bottom of the glass. When you used the potting soil, you didn't see any bubbles. Plants growing in soil act like a "glue" and help hold the soil together. If the plant life is destroyed or removed, the soil falls apart and becomes dirt. Potting soil doesn't have plants to help it stick together, so it doesn't hold much air. The reason gardeners and farmers "aerate" or poke holes in the soil is because over time soils can become compacted or packed down, leaving very little space for the air and water plants need for growth.

22. Full of Holes

You've seen that soil is full of air, and that different soils can contain different amounts of air and water, but how does this happen?

You Will Need

- a 500 mL (2 cup) measuring cup
- a 500 mL (2 cup) plastic drinking glass
- marbles
- sand
- water

What to Do

1. Fill your measuring cup with marbles. Pour the marbles into a plastic drinking glass. Is it full?

2. Fill the measuring cup with sand. Pour the sand over top of the marbles, tapping the glass gently until as much sand as possible is in the cup. How much sand is left over? Is the glass full? Remove the extra sand from the measuring cup.

3. Fill the measuring cup with water. Pour the water over the sand and marbles in the drinking glass until as much water as possible is in the cup. How much water is left over? Is the glass full?

WHAT HAPPENED?

You were able to add more of the materials to the cup even though it seemed to be full each time. If you looked carefully after you added the water, you may have seen air bubbles. Sandy soils are like the marbles, with lots of spaces between the particles to add additional materials such as air or water. Soils made with more silt or clay have smaller spaces between the particles, which makes it more difficult for water to stay in the soil. If soil is clay, with few spaces, no roots can develop. If it is too sandy, it won't be able to hold the nutrients plants need to grow. It is always important for farmers to know what kind of soil they have so they can make sure to plant in the best areas.

23. Clay Baking

Terracotta or "baked earth" is the term used to describe certain items made of clay. People have been using clay for over 5,000 years to make sculptures, cooking vessels and building materials. While you won't be making a brick oven, you can bake with clay.

You Will Need

- an adult helper
- an oven
- 2 baking apples like Cortland, Fuji or Gala
- 2 mL (½ tsp) cinnamon
- 5 mL (1 tsp) lemon juice
- 2 small pitas
- measuring spoons
- a bowl
- a knife
- parchment paper bags (not brown paper bags) or parchment paper
- low-fire earthenware clay (available at art stores)
- 10 mL (2 tsp) sugar
- oven mitts
- cookie shet
- a hammer

NOTE: Be sure to ONLY use earthenware clay, NOT air-dry clay, polymer clay such as Sculpey, or other forms of modelling clay.

What to Do

1. Preheat oven to 175 °C (350 °F).

2. Have an adult dice the apples. Put them into a bowl and add 10 mL (2 tsp) of sugar and 2 mL (½ tsp) of cinnamon to the bowl. Toss to mix, then add 5 mL (1 tsp) of lemon juice to the apple mixture.

3. Have an adult cut a small slit in the pitas. Stuff the apple mixture into each pita.

4. Place each pita in a parchment paper bag and tightly fold the ends of the bag. If using parchment paper, take each of the long ends of the paper and join them above the pita. Fold the edges over so that it is sealed. Fold the paper a second time and then lie it on top of the pita. Take the two short sides and fold over.

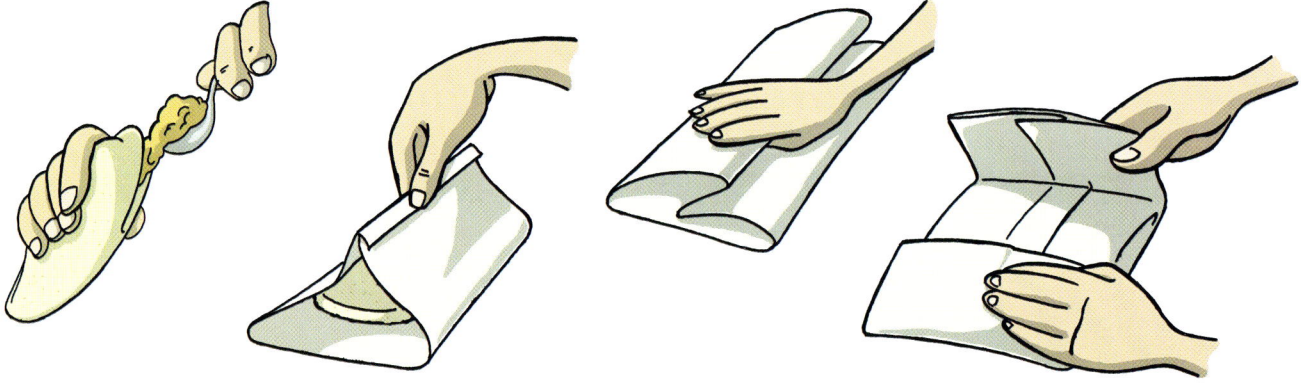

44

5. Roll out the clay so that it is about ½ cm (¼ in) thick, and wide enough to wrap around one of the covered pitas.

6. Place one of the sealed pita apples on the clay, and fold the clay over the food pocket. Pinch the ends of the clay to completely seal the pocket. Place both pitas on an ungreased cookie sheet.

7. Have an adult put both pitas into the oven and bake for about 40 minutes or until the clay has hardened. Don't worry if the clay has cracked.

8. Have an adult remove the pitas from the oven. After they have cooled, use a hammer to break open the clay container. When both pitas have cooled, examine and taste them. Were there any differences?

WHAT HAPPENED?

The pita pocket that was baked in the clay was moist, while the one baked just in parchment was crispy. The clay keeps the moisture and heat in the packet so the pita remains moist. Clay baking has been used by people throughout the world as a way to prepare food. In many cultures, fish or poultry are roasted in clay, either in ovens or in open fires. Clay has been used for thousands of years to make containers for cooking or storing food and water. Clay is also used to make bricks and tiles for building and to make beautiful sculptures.

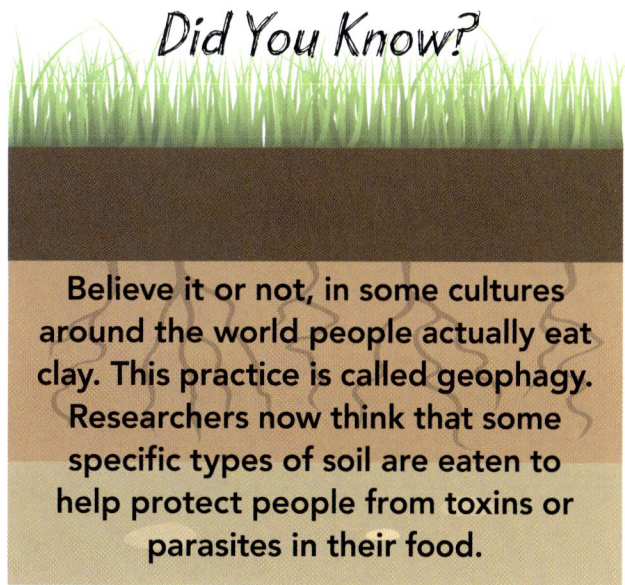

Did You Know?

Believe it or not, in some cultures around the world people actually eat clay. This practice is called geophagy. Researchers now think that some specific types of soil are eaten to help protect people from toxins or parasites in their food.

24. Rolling Stones

What do a jar of mixed nuts and a garden in spring have in common? Here's a science trick that will help explain why rocks that weren't in your garden in the fall mysteriously appear after the snow melts.

You Will Need

- a clear plastic jar with a lid (a small peanut butter jar is perfect)
- rice
- a walnut in the shell

What to Do

1. Place the walnut in the bottom of the jar.
2. Fill the jar with rice and place the lid on the jar.
3. Hold the jar upright in one hand and tap the bottom of the jar against the palm of your other hand.
4. After about 10 taps, open the lid of the jar. Where is the walnut?
5. Put the lid back on the jar and turn the jar upside down. Can you make the walnut return to the bottom of the jar?

WHAT HAPPENED?

The walnut rose to the top of the jar. Each time you tapped the jar, grains of rice were loosened, allowing them to move down and around the walnut. As they moved beneath the walnut, they moved it and pushed it upward. In the spring you find rocks and boulders have risen to the earth's surface. As the ground freezes and thaws, it loosens dirt. This dirt then moves down and around rocks and boulders, pushing them toward the surface of the garden. The same thing happens in a can of mixed nuts. Scientists call this The Brazil Nut Effect. If you tap an unopened can of nuts the same way you did in step 3 above, you would find all the large nuts, like Brazil nuts, have risen to the top of the can, leaving the smaller nuts, like peanuts, at the bottom.

25. Survival 101

Do you think you can collect water without an obvious source of water like a lake or stream nearby? This next activity will show you how soil can help ease your thirst!

You Will Need

- an adult helper
- a garden
- a warm day
- a shovel or trowel
- a disposable cup
- plastic wrap
- small rocks

What to Do

1. Ask an adult for permission before you begin digging a hole. Find a flat, sunny spot in the garden and use a shovel or trowel to dig a hole 20 cm x 20 cm (8 in x 8 in) wide and about 20 cm (8 in) deep. Leave this hole open overnight.
2. Early the next morning, place a disposable cup facing upward in the hole.
3. Cover the top of the hole with a piece of plastic wrap about 28 cm x 28 cm (11 in x 11 in). Use rocks and stones around the edges to keep the plastic wrap in place.
4. Place a small rock or stone on the plastic wrap, so the stone is centred over the opening of the cup. The plastic wrap should form a cone-shape over the cup.
5. Leave this overnight.
6. The next morning check on the cup. What did you find inside?

WHAT HAPPENED?

In the morning you found water in the cup. The air in the soil is quite humid. This means it contains lots of water vapour. During the day the heat of the sun causes more of the water in the soil to **evaporate** and form more water vapour. When the air cools at night this water vapour condenses and changes back into liquid water. The plastic traps the water that evaporates and then condenses. When there is enough liquid water condensing on the plastic, the water forms drops that drip down to the lowest point, below the rock. When enough drops fall into the cup you have filled it with water.

Glossary

Acid: a sour substance that forms water and a salt when mixed with a base

Adsorbed: collected particles of a substance on a surface

Alkaline: containing a base

Anthocyanin: coloured pigments found in plants

Bacteria: tiny microorganisms that are usually one-celled

Base: a bitter substance that forms water and a salt when mixed with an acid

Clay: soil composed of mineral particles of very small size

Compost: a mixture of decomposing plant matter used to fertilize and improve soil

Dirt: the non-living components of soil such as clay, sand and silt

Drought: a long period of dry weather

Evaporate: to change in state from a liquid to a gas

Fertilizer: any material put on soil to improve its ability to grow plants

Fungi: a group of living things that live on decaying matter; includes mushrooms, moulds and mildews

Humus: the part of soil made from decayed plant and animal matter

Hydroponic: the science of growing plants in a nutrient-rich solution without soil

Loam: nutrient-rich soil made of clay, silt, sand and organic material

Minerals: pure inorganic substances that form rocks

Neutral: neither acidic nor alkaline

Organic materials: living matter such as the plant material and microorganisms in soil

pH: a measure of acidity; high pH values indicate a base, low values an acid. A pH of 7 is considered neutral

Pigments: coloured chemicals

Soil: the surface layer of the earth containing both inorganic and organic materials to support plant growth

Weathering: the breakdown of rocks and soil. Can be caused by chemical or mechanical means